First
1000 Words

How to use this book

Small children love looking at pictures and naming what they see. It can be even more fun if they share a word book with a grown-up. You could start by talking about what is going on in the big pictures. There will be many things that your child will recognize, as well as new objects to discuss.

On pages with small pictures around the edge, children will enjoy finding each image in the large picture. It is useful to talk about the colors and shapes they are looking for, as the scal e of the object may be very different in each place.

Rhymes at the bottom of each page encourage children to look more closely at the pictures and to talk about their own experience. Finally, they are asked to find Teddy Bear (who appears on the cover of this book) wherever he is hiding!

As children gain confidence, they will enjoy finding objects throughout the book, not just on one page. Later on, you can introduce them to the Word List at the back, showing them that it is arranged alphabetically.

One of the best ways to help your child enjoy books and reading is to show that you enjoy them, too. We hope you both have fun with this book!

Teddy Bear's
Fun to Learn

First
1000 Words

Written by Nicola Baxter

Illustrated by Susie Lacome

ARMADILLO

This hardback edition published in 2006
by Armadillo Books
An imprint of Bookmart Limited
Registered Number 2372865
Trading as Bookmart Limited
Blaby Road, Wigston
Leicestershire, LE18 4SE, England

ISBN: 1-84322-253-1

3 5 7 9 10 8 6 4 2

Produced for Bookmart Ltd by
Nicola Baxter
PO Box 215, Framingham Earl,
Norwich NR14 7UR

Editorial Consultant: Ronne Randall
Designer: Amanda Hawkes

Printed in Singapore

Contents

At Home

trash can

bucket

tool box

window box

roof

pipe

path

chimney

ladder

window

door

Uncle Ted is working hard,
Fixing a loose tile.
What might be be listening to
That brings a happy smile?

radio

 doorstep

 Thermos

 lunch box

 bricks

 roof tile

 trellis

 security light

 driveway

 doorbell

 napkin

 antenna

 glove

Can you see two yellow gloves
For Uncle Ted to wear?
What is in his tool box?
And where's that Teddy Bear?

The Kitchen

 measuring cup

 saucepan

cookbook

 toaster

 rolling pin

 canister

refrigerator

 wooden spoon

 frying pan

 dish towel

 microwave

Someone's busy helping
His mommy make a cake.
Can you see how big a mess
A little bear can make?

counter

 stool

 stove

 kettle

 iron

 sink

 food mixer

 dishwashing liquid

 drawer

 bulletin board

 dishwasher

 drainboard

 mixing bowl

Where is the saucepan lid?
How many spoons are there?
What is in the open drawer?
And where is Teddy Bear?

9

The Bedroom

 hairbrush comforter mobile comb

bed

armoire

chest of drawers

night table

pajamas

bathrobe

pillow

Here is Teddy's bedroom
And Teddy's little bed.
How many things
Can you see that are red?

10

slippers

 socks

 toy box

 poster

 kite

comic book

 light

 height chart

 wastebasket

 alarm clock

 painting

 hanger

 money box

Can you find both Teddy's socks
To make a perfect pair?
What's that on his comforter?
And where is Teddy Bear?

11

The Bathroom

 soap washcloth sponge toothbrush

bathtub

washstand

toilet paper

shower

shower curtain

bath mat

cabinet

When a bear's been doing painting
He's never very clean.
If you follow colored pawprints
You can see just where he's been.

12

toilet
 mirror
 nail brush
 faucet
 scale
towel
 shampoo

 bubble bath

 toothpaste

 toy boat

 wall tiles

 back brush

 rubber duck

Yes, Teddy Bear's left pawprints
Almost everywhere.
Can you see a purple print?
And where is Teddy Bear?

The Living Room

rug

armchair

bookcase

magazine

vacuum
cleaner

plant

dust cloth

Someone's very busy
Cleaning up the living room.
Can you see three dustcloths
And the end of a broom?

newspaper vase VCR photograph carpet picture table

 remote control

 sofa

 fireplace

 television

 stereo

 wallpaper

How many flowers
In the vase are there?
What's in the fireplace?
And where is Teddy Bear?

The Attic

cradle

dollhouse

cage

skylight

cardboard box

picture frame

suitcase

dressmaker's dummy

skis

light bulb

spider web

There may be treasures in the attic
As every teddy knows.
What can you see that would
Be useful when it snows?

16

paint
 deck chair
 bottles
 sun hat
 jars
 trapdoor
 fishing rod

 rocking chair

decorations

sewing machine

 rocking horse

 ice skates

And what could you use
When the sun is shining bright?
Can you count the jars?
And is Teddy Bear in sight?

 sled

The Yard

 fork

 grass

 lawn mower

 seeds

 wheelbarrow

 shears

 soil

 spade

 flowerpot

 watering can

 hose

In this lovely yard
Many plants and flowers grow.
But what comes tumbling from the tree
When strong winds blow?

18

leaves

 birdhouse

 hoe

 hand fork

 trowel

 bird feeder

shed

 hanging basket

 rake

 hedge

 flowers

birdbath

 broom

After hard work in the sunshine,
The yard is at its best.
Can you spot that Teddy Bear
Taking a well-earned rest?

The Street

 bicycle

 pigeon

candy

 cake

 sidewalk

 iron fence

 streetlight

 litter basket

 delivery van

 driver

 stroller

The street is always busy.
How many bears can you spy?
Have you spotted anything
That **you** would like to buy?

20

school
 bakery
 package
 street
 lollipop
 drain
safety helmet

shopping bag

shoe store

street sign

candy store

jump rope

boots

Main Street

Where could you find some slippers,
Or a cinnamon bun?
Can you see that Teddy Bear
Having lots of fun?

21

The Supermarket

change purse money fruit purse

cans

shopper

shopping cart

line

basket

shopping bag

cash register

Do you like shopping?
Teddy thinks it's fine!
How many shoppers
Are standing in the line?

22

milk
 keys
 yogurt
 carton
 juice
 honey
 bar code

 salesclerk

 receipt

 sign

 cashier

 vegetables

 conveyor belt

How many teddies
Wearing blue are there?
Can you find the carrots?
Can you see that Teddy Bear?

At School

 teacher   felt-tip pens   paper   water jar

ruler

chalkboard

map

crayons

modeling clay

chalk

coat hooks

There's so much to do
At Teddy's nursery school.
But coming in late
Is against the rule!

24

pupil paintbrush eraser portrait aquarium easel paintbox

alphabet

notebook

computer

schoolbag

puzzle

scissors

a b c d e
f g h i j k l
m n o p q
r s t u v w
x y z

How many girls
Have bows in their hair?
Who's making pawprints?
And where's that Teddy Bear?

On the Move

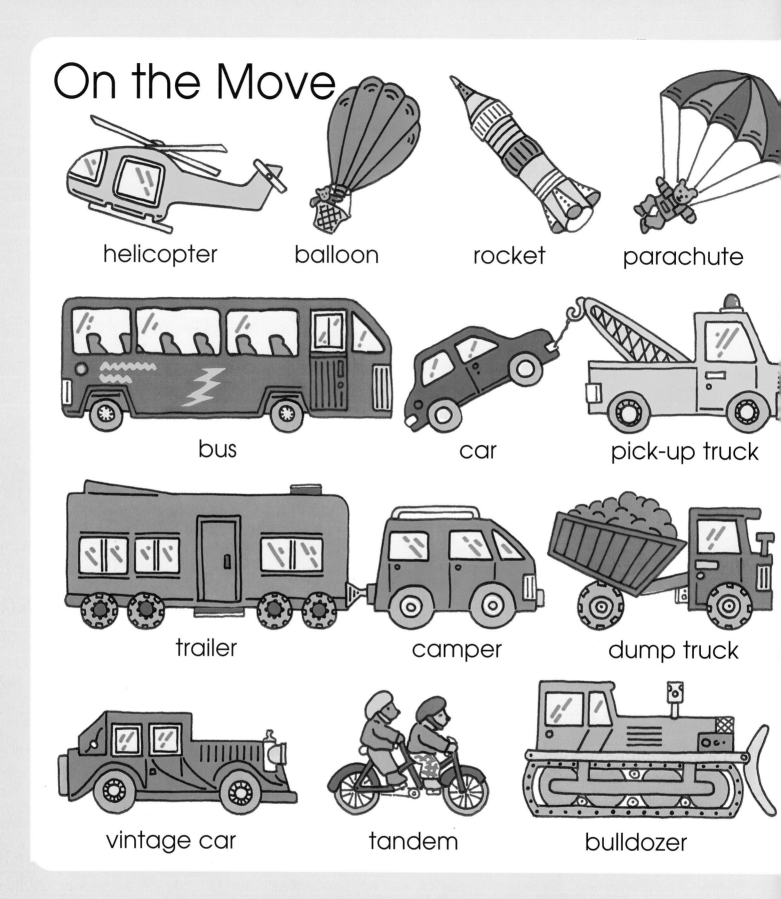

helicopter

balloon

rocket

parachute

bus

car

pick-up truck

trailer

camper

dump truck

vintage car

tandem

bulldozer

How many wheels
Can you see here?
Which of the vehicles
Would be hardest to steer?

racing car

steamroller

garbage truck

tractor-trailer

go-cart

truck

motorcycle

tanker

power shovel

auto carrier

moving van

Which vehicle is oldest?
(It's really very rare.)
Which could travel farthest?
And where's that Teddy Bear?

The Farm

sheep   lamb   pig   piglet

chicks

hen

dog

horse

foal

farmer

farmhouse

Here's a busy farmer.
What's that in his hand?
Can you name the animals
That live on his land?

duck
 duckling
 cat
 mouse
 gate
 fence
 scarecrow

 pond

 rooster

 cow

 calf

 field

 tractor

Who's in the duck pond?
How many chicks are there?
Who's that rolling in the mud?
And where is Teddy Bear?

The Park

ice cream

slide

swing

jogger

sandbox

fountain

flower bed

bench

knee pads

bird

horn

In the park one sunny day
Teddy bears are having fun.
How many are there?
Can you count them, one by one?

tricycle
 skateboard
 seesaw
 wheels
 picnic basket
 hoop
 ball

 picnic

 squirrel

 sandwiches

 scooter

 roller skates

 cassette player

How many bears
On wheels are there?
What is in the basket?
And where is Teddy Bear?

31

Storybook World

wishing well   toadstool   elf   fairy

wand

lance   shield   crown

sword

armor

dragon   knight   princess

Can you tell a story
About everything you see?
Who can do **real** magic?
Who is brave as he can be?

banner

top hat

page

pumpkin

magician

prince

queen

king

cloak

giant

castle

Do you know the names for clothes
That knights and princes wear?
Who lost a glass slipper?
Can you spot our Teddy Bear?

The Country

 tent

 tree

 hiker

 bridge

 woods

 mountain

 meadow

 river

 lake

 branch

campfire

The country is so beautiful,
A lovely place to be.
How many green things
Can you see?

trunk train engine train car bush binoculars waterfall log

village

railroad track

rowboat

hill

sleeping bag

rocks

Can you count two flowers?
Can you see a little train?
Does the village have a church?
Find Teddy Bear again!

35

The Harbor

 fish
 paddle
 rope
 buoy

portholes

submarine

ocean liner

fisherman

crane

fishing boat

motorboat

Here's a busy harbor.
Which is your favorite boat?
Which things are supposed to sink
And which are supposed to float?

36

life jacket
 hook
 anchor
 lobster
 mast
canoe
water-skier

 lobster pot

 wet suit

 jetty

 container ship

 diver

 life preserver

The back of a boat is called the stern.
The front is called the bow.
Our Teddy's holding a paddle.
Can you see him now?

The Airport

cane

milkshake

luggage cart

arrivals board

airport bus

airplane

control tower

restrooms

hangar

label

clipboard

At this busy airport,
Traveling teddies come and go.
Where's the public telephone?
What does a pilot do?

briefcase

 coffee

 runway

 broom

 cleaner

 tickets

 camera

 windsock

pilot

 check-in

 flight attendant

 backpack

 telephone

Is the weather very windy?
Who keeps the airport clean?
And is our little Teddy Bear
Anywhere to be seen?

The Hospital

 tray   nurse   water   bandage

sheet

doctor

nightgown

medicine

visitor

walker

cotton balls

When a teddy's feeling poorly
Or has taken a bad fall,
She'll get better in the hospital
In no time at all.

elevator

 porter

 watch

sling

adhesive bandage

hypodermic syringe

 blanket

 get-well card

 plaster cast

 temperature chart

 stethoscope

 thermometer

 wheelchair

Can you see a visitor
With presents for sick bears?
And can you spot our Teddy Bear,
Who didn't climb the stairs?

All at Sea

 pirate flag

 seahorse

chain

pearl

 whale

galleon

 message in a bottle

 shark

 swimmer

 treasure chest

 jellyfish

Ahoy there, teddy bears!
What treasures can you spy,
Down at the bottom of the sea,
Where the jellyfish floats by?

coral
 octopus
 pirate
 dolphin
 pistol
 eye patch
 oyster

 treasure map

 keyhole

 island

 seaweed

 mermaid

 palm tree

What is on the pirate flag?
How many shells can you see?
Who has got the treasure map?
And where can Teddy Bear be?

43

The Toy Store

abacus   bowling   fort   doll

tea set

Jack-in-the-box

colored pencils

top

playhouse

board game

hand puppet

Teddy loves the toy store.
It's a super place to play.
Which toy would you like to have
If you could choose today?

44

beads

wagon

yo-yo

dice

marbles

robot

stacking cups

blocks

pull toy

soldiers

coloring book

pedal car

dressing-up costume

How can the storekeeper
Reach the highest shelf?
And where has little Teddy Bear
Hidden himself?

The Workshop

 wrench

 flashlight

 mug

 drill

pocket

calendar

shelf

doorknob

measuring
tape

cookies

Noah's ark

Someone's helping Uncle Ted
To make a Noah's Ark.
Which tool would be useful
For seeing in the dark?

46

saw
 screwdriver
 screws
 nails
 hammer
 goggles
 penknife

 sandpaper

 mallet

 plank

 animals

 pliers

 workbench

What is our teddy holding?
What are those goggles for?
Which other animals could Ted make?
What color is the door?

The Beach

 flag

 sand

sea shell

 ocean

 sandcastle

starfish

 bathing suit

beach umbrella

 pebbles

 fishing net

 sunglasses

Days at the beach are always fun,
With water, sun, and sand.
Look! What's the teddy in the chair
Holding in her hand?

crab

 flippers

 sailboat

 water wings

 sun

waves

 sunscreen

 lighthouse

 rubber tube

 beachball

 swimming trunks

 sea gull

 ice pop

How do the bears make extra sure
They're not burned by the sun?
How many sea shells can you see?
Where's our Teddy having fun?

Party Time

 present
 clown
 candle
 button

 straw

 party hat

 piece of cake

 soda pop

 paper cup

 tablecloth

 birthday cake

Happy Birthday, Teddy Tim!
How old are your today?
Lots of friends have come to share
Your very special day.

vest

ribbon

balloon

bow tie

mask

bow

blindfold

wrapping paper

streamers

party bag

envelope

birthday card

party dress

How many bears are wearing hats?
How many presents are there?
How many balls are in the air?
Can you spot our Teddy Bear?

Parts of the Body

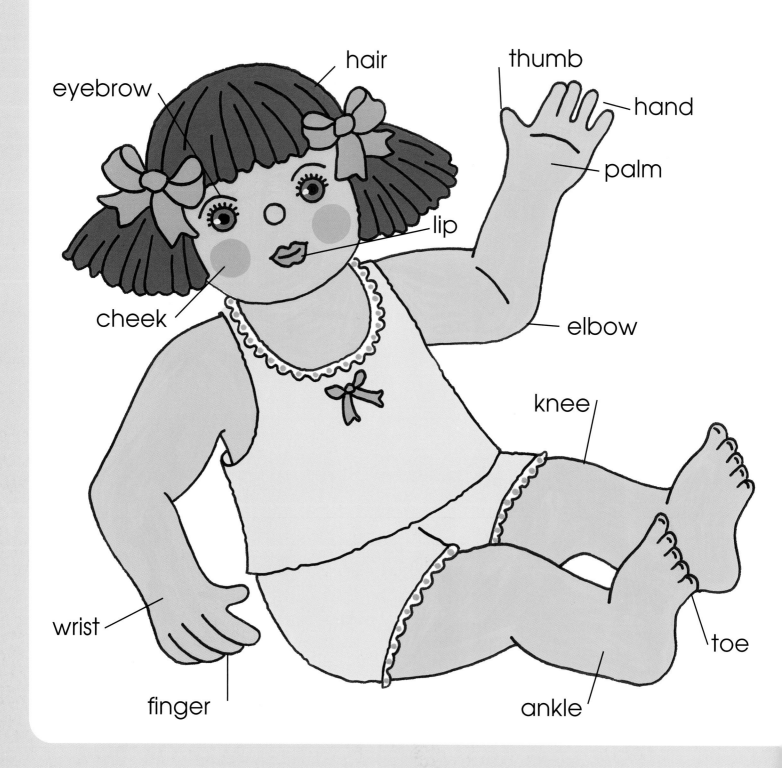

eyebrow

hair

thumb

hand

palm

lip

cheek

elbow

knee

wrist

finger

ankle

toe

Can you count Dolly's fingers?
Can you count her toes?
Can you put **your** finger
On her little button nose?

head

ear

eye

mouth

paw

nose

shoulder

arm

foot

stomach

back

leg

bottom

Dolly's eyes are brightest brown.
Teddy's eyes are blue.
What color are **your** lovely eyes?
Can you name each part of **you**?

Busy Teddies

crawling	sitting	reading	cuddling
singing	drinking	eating	writing
waving	washing	drying	sleeping

What a lot of busy teddies!
Can you copy what they do?
What is one teddy eating?
Who is using pink shampoo?

kicking

jumping

riding

hopping

walking

dressing

running

jumping rope

pushing

pulling

dancing

standing

What is the standing teddy holding?
Who needs another sock to wear?
What is one teddy kicking?
Can you see that Teddy Bear?

Seasons

spring

summer

fall

winter

The year is always changing.
Which season is it now?
Our bear has fun all year round—
Can you tell me how?

Weather

sunshine

snow

rainbow

ice

hurricane

icicles

wind

snowflake

cloud

tornado

snowman

rain

dew

lightning

hot

flood

frost

fog

cold

puddles

Look out of the window.
What's the weather like today?
What kind of weather is the best
For going out to play?

Favorite Food

butter

cracker

cereal

sugar

soup

hot dog

fries

sauces

chocolate

rice

doughnuts

spaghetti

Here are Teddy's favorite foods.
What do you like to eat?
Which of these foods are savory
And which of them are sweet?

salad

hamburger

pizza

baked beans

muffin

cheese

bread

sausages

nuts

flour

omelet

pie

Can you see what happens
When Teddy helps to bake?
When you help in the kitchen
What do you like to make?

Sports and Games

cricket

baseball

football

tennis

high jump

archery

three-legged race

climbing

diving

pole vaulting

team

gymnastics

Here are lots of teddies!
Have you tried these sports?
How many bears are jumping high?
Which ones are wearing shorts?

trampolining   bicycling   weightlifting   rowing

roller skating   golf   soccer   sack race

ice skating   basketball   martial arts   trophy

Why might you get a trophy?
Does it matter if you win?
Which teddy has a target?
Which race is Teddy Bear in?

Music, Please!

tambourine

triangle

cymbals

maracas

violin

keyboard

trombone

recorder

music stand

notes

conductor

cello

Can you play an instrument?
Do you like to dance and sing?
Which instruments go toot-de-toot?
And which goes ting-a-ling?

flute

music

oboe

trumpet

saxophone

banjo

xylophone

guitar

harp

piano

kettledrums

Which instruments do you have to blow?
Which ones do you bang or shake?
Do you know what a conductor does?
What difference does he make?

Baby Bears

rattle

bib

baby bottle

pacifier

bootees

baby alarm

changing mat

baby record book

bank

sleeper

crib

Twin babies keep you busy!
Teddy's helping out today.
Where is one baby's bunny?
What is she throwing away?

baby
carriage

baby
blanket

diaper

tissues

teething ring

potty

high chair

training cup

cloth book

board book

bunny

mattress

diaper bag

Why do babies sleep in special beds
And sit in special chairs?
Can you remember when you were
As small as these baby bears?

Numbers

one house

two cars

three kites

four rabbits

five balloons

six ducks

seven strawberries

eight crayons

nine flowers

ten hearts

Can you count from one to ten?
How many flowers can you see?
Can you count from ten to one?
How many kites are flying free?

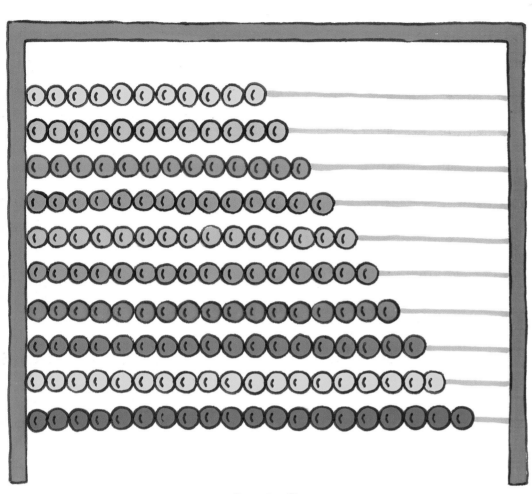

11 eleven
12 twelve
13 thirteen
14 fourteen
15 fifteen
16 sixteen
17 seventeen
18 eighteen
19 nineteen
20 twenty

100 one hundred

third   second   first

How many beads are colored green?
How many are colored blue?
Will our Teddy win his race?
Can you count to one hundred too?

Colors

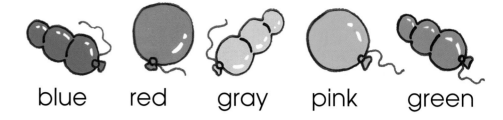

blue   red   gray   pink   green

white

black

yellow

brown

purple

orange

navy

Look at all the big balloons
That Teddy's holding tight!
Which is your favorite colour?
Is it pale or is it bright?

68

Shapes

 heart   stripes   circle   square   star diamond

rectangle

zigzags

dots

oval

triangle

checks

Teddy's painted lots of shapes
With patterns in between.
What has Teddy painted red?
Which shape is colored green?

69

Clothes

hat   handkerchief   mittens   sneakers

scarf

jeans

jacket

blouse

undershirt

pants

sweater

70

Teddy's hanging lots of clothes
On the line to dry.
Who do you think helped
To hang the rest so high?

parka

 boots

 shorts

 skirt

 underpants

T-shirt

clothespin

 shoes

 overalls

shirt

 coat

 tie

 tights

Which clothes might be Teddy's own?
Which would you like to wear?
Have you got as many clothes
As lucky Teddy Bear?

Families

great-grandmother   great-grandfather

grandmother   grandfather   great-aunt   great-uncle

father   mother   aunt   uncle

sister   Teddy Bear   brother   cousin   twins

Here is Teddy's family.
He's waving—can you see?
Who are all the people
On your family tree?

Feelings

scared

happy

shy

embarrassed

bored

angry

thoughtful

sad

proud

sorry

How are these teddies feeling?
What has made a teddy cry?
Why is another teddy sorry?
Have you ever felt shy?

Fruits

raspberry

grapes

blueberries

fig

mango

rhubarb

kiwi

pear   banana   watermelon

lime

The bowl is full of juicy fruit!
What would you choose to eat?
Which fruits can taste a little sharp
And which are always sweet?

orange

peach

lemon

plum

apricot

cherry

apple

papaya

grapefruit

strawberry

cranberries

tangerine

pineapple

Can you always eat the skin?
How many strawberries are there?
Which fruit is just about to be
Eaten by Teddy Bear?

75

Vegetables

mushrooms

carrot

broccoli

red pepper

peas

leek

corn

onion

potato

cauliflower

tomatoes

celery

Vegetables are good to eat.
Which ones have you tasted?
What is Teddy munching,
Making sure that none is wasted?

lettuce

beet

lima beans

parsnip

cucumber

radishes

sweet potato

green beans

turnip

herbs

cabbage

zucchini

Which vegetables need to be cooked?
Which ones can you eat raw?
Which do you like to eat so much
You always ask for more?

Flowers

poppy

iris

daisy

bluebell

pansy

daffodil

dahlia

sunflower

carnation

lily

rose

Which flowers are yellow?
Which flowers are blue?
And which can grow
Even taller than you?

Time to Eat!

 teaspoon pepper salt saucer cup

 plate

 knife

 fork

 spoon

 place mat

 glass

 pitcher

Teddy is setting the table.
What is he holding up?
And what do you often find
Underneath a cup?

Opposites

slow   fast   big   little

tall   short   open   shut

on   off   bottom   top

Are you bigger than an elephant?
Are you smaller than a mouse?
Do you go to sleep at night
Outside or inside your house?

up

down

old

new

full

empty

light

heavy

inside

outside

thin

fat

Are you young or are you old?
Are you a girl or boy?
And can you see that Teddy Bear
With a favorite toy?

Birds

feather

nest

egg

beak

wing

owl

puffin

toucan

penguin

peacock

ostrich

emu

Do you know which of these birds
Never fly at all?
Which ones love to eat a fish?
Which one is very tall?

kingfisher   swallow   kiwi   hummingbird

albatross   vulture   goose   turkey

flamingo   pelican   stork   swan

What noise does a turkey make?
What about an owl?
Can you see where Teddy Bear
Is feeding a waterfowl?

Minibeasts

 bee

 snail

 ladybug

 lizard

worm

butterfly

wasp

caterpillar

beetle

millipede

chameleon

Which minibeasts can creep or crawl?
Which ones hop or fly?
Which ones can be hard to see
If you walk quickly by?

moth   ant   grasshopper   slug   fly   flea   chrysalis

walking stick

tarantula

frog

centipede

dragonfly

spider

Which minibeasts can sting or bite?
Why do you think they do?
And can you spot that Teddy Bear
Watching them—and you?

Wild Animals

koala rhinoceros armadillo kangaroo

polar bear gorilla giraffe monkey

tiger elephant snake panda

Can you see an animal
Who moves along by jumping?
Can you see another one
Who gives his chest a thumping?

raccoon

buffalo

porcupine

zebra

bear

crocodile

camel

lion

wolf

leopard

beaver

hippopotamus

Who has lots of prickles?
Who lives in a lair?
And who is being fed
By a kindly Teddy Bear?

Animal Friends

doghouse kitten hamster hutch

canary

rabbit

parrot

parakeet

guinea pig

pet food

goldfish

Who lives in a doghouse?
Who has a special door?
What color is the parrot?
What is that small brush for?

puppy
 bubbles
 brush
 tortoise
 bone
 leash
 collar

dog bowl

cat basket

fish tank

cat flap

turtle

water bowl

How many bubbles
In the fish tank are there?
And what tasty rabbit snack
Is being held by Teddy Bear?

Word List

a

abacus	44
adhesive bandage	41
airplane	38
airport bus	38
alarm clock	11
albatross	83
alphabet	25
anchor	37
angry	73
animals	47
ankle	52
ant	85
antenna	7
apple	75
apricot	75
aquarium	25
archery	60
arm	53
armadillo	86
armchair	14
armoire	10
armor	32
arrivals board	38
aunt	72
auto carrier	27

b

baby alarm	64
baby blanket	65
baby bottle	64
baby carriage	65
baby record book	64
back	53
back brush	13

backpack	25, 39
baked beans	59
bakery	21
ball	31
balloon	26, 51
banana	74
bandage	40
bank	64
banjo	63
banner	33
bar code	23
baseball	60
basket	22
basketball	61
bathing suit	48
bath mat	12
bathrobe	10
bathtub	12
beachball	49
beach umbrella	48
beads	45
beak	82
bear	87
beaver	87
bed	10
bee	84
beet	77
beetle	84
bench	30
bib	64
bicycle	20
bicycling	61
big	80
binoculars	35
bird	30
birdbath	19
bird feeder	19
birdhouse	19
birthday cake	50
birthday card	51

black	68
blanket	41
blindfold	51
blocks	45
blouse	70
blue	68
bluebell	78
blueberries	74
board book	65
board game	44
bone	89
bookcase	14
bootees	64
boots	21
boots	71
bored	73
bottles	17
bottom	53
bottom	80
bow	51
bowling	44
bow tie	51
branch	34
bread	59
bricks	7
bridge	34
briefcase	39
broccoli	76
broom	19
brother	72
brown	68
brush	89
bubble bath	13
bubbles	89
bucket	6
buffalo	87
bulldozer	26
bulletin board	9
bunny	65
buoy	36

bus	26
bush	35
butter	58
butterfly	84
button	50

c

cabbage	77
cabinet	12
cage	16
cake	20
calendar	46
calf	29
camel	87
camera	39
campfire	34
camper	26
canary	88
candle	50
candy	20
candy store	21
cane	38
canister	8
canoe	37
cans	22
car	26
cardboard box	16
carnation	78
carpet	15
carrot	76
carton	23
cashier	23
cash register	22
cassette player	31
castle	33
cat	29
cat basket	89
cat flap	89
caterpillar	84

93